SIMPLE

SERMON
NOTES

FOR TEENS

ISBN: 1540571823
ISBN-13: 978-1540571823

TOPIC/TITLE: _____

DATE: _____ **SPEAKER:** _____

SCRIPTURE: _____

Keyword:	Prayer Requests:
_____	_____
	_____
	_____
	_____

MAIN POINTS OR "WOW!" STATEMENTS:

1
_____
_____
_____
_____
_____
_____

2
_____
_____
_____
_____
_____
_____

3
_____
_____
_____
_____
_____
_____

NOTES:

_____
_____
_____
_____
_____
_____
_____
_____
_____
_____
_____
_____
_____
_____
_____
_____
_____
_____
_____
_____
_____
_____
_____
_____
_____
_____

TODAY'S SERMON ENCOURAGED ME TO:

_____
_____
_____

TOPIC/TITLE: _____

DATE: _____ **SPEAKER:** _____

SCRIPTURE: _____

Keyword:
_____

Prayer Requests:
_____
_____
_____
_____

MAIN POINTS OR "WOW!" STATEMENTS:

1
_____
_____
_____
_____
_____

2
_____
_____
_____
_____
_____

3
_____
_____
_____
_____
_____

NOTES:

_____

_____

_____

_____

_____

_____

_____

_____

_____

_____

_____

_____

_____

_____

_____

_____

_____

_____

_____

_____

_____

_____

_____

TODAY'S SERMON ENCOURAGED ME TO:

_____

_____

_____

TOPIC/TITLE: _____

DATE: _____ **SPEAKER:** _____

SCRIPTURE: _____

Keyword:
_____

Prayer Requests:
_____
_____
_____
_____

MAIN POINTS OR "WOW!" STATEMENTS:

1
_____
_____
_____
_____

2
_____
_____
_____
_____

3
_____
_____
_____
_____

NOTES:

_____

_____

_____

_____

_____

_____

_____

_____

_____

_____

_____

_____

_____

_____

_____

_____

_____

_____

_____

_____

_____

_____

_____

_____

TODAY'S SERMON ENCOURAGED ME TO:

_____

_____

_____

TOPIC/TITLE: _____

DATE: _____ **SPEAKER:** _____

SCRIPTURE: _____

Keyword:	Prayer Requests:
_____	_____ _____ _____ _____

MAIN POINTS OR "WOW!" STATEMENTS:

1
_____
_____
_____
_____
_____

2
_____
_____
_____
_____
_____

3
_____
_____
_____
_____
_____

NOTES:

_____
_____
_____
_____
_____
_____
_____
_____
_____
_____
_____
_____
_____
_____
_____
_____
_____
_____
_____
_____
_____
_____
_____
_____

TODAY'S SERMON ENCOURAGED ME TO:

_____
_____
_____

TOPIC/TITLE: _____

DATE: _____ **SPEAKER:** _____

SCRIPTURE: _____

Keyword:

_____

Prayer Requests:

_____
_____
_____
_____

MAIN POINTS OR "WOW!" STATEMENTS:

1
_____
_____
_____
_____
_____

2
_____
_____
_____
_____
_____

3
_____
_____
_____
_____
_____

NOTES:

_____
_____
_____
_____
_____
_____
_____
_____
_____
_____
_____
_____
_____
_____
_____
_____
_____
_____
_____
_____
_____
_____
_____
_____
_____

TODAY'S SERMON ENCOURAGED ME TO:

_____
_____
_____

TOPIC/TITLE: _____

DATE: _____ **SPEAKER:** _____

SCRIPTURE: _____

Keyword:

_____

Prayer Requests:

_____
_____
_____
_____

MAIN POINTS OR "WOW!" STATEMENTS:

1

_____
_____
_____
_____
_____

2

_____
_____
_____
_____
_____

3

_____
_____
_____
_____
_____

NOTES:

_____

_____

_____

_____

_____

_____

_____

_____

_____

_____

_____

_____

_____

_____

_____

_____

_____

_____

_____

_____

_____

_____

_____

_____

_____

_____

TODAY'S SERMON ENCOURAGED ME TO:

_____

_____

_____

TOPIC/TITLE: _____

DATE: _____ **SPEAKER:** _____

SCRIPTURE: _____

Keyword:

_____

Prayer Requests:
_____
_____
_____
_____

MAIN POINTS OR "WOW!" STATEMENTS:

1
_____
_____
_____
_____
_____

2
_____
_____
_____
_____
_____

3
_____
_____
_____
_____
_____

NOTES:

_____

_____

_____

_____

_____

_____

_____

_____

_____

_____

_____

_____

_____

_____

_____

_____

_____

_____

_____

_____

_____

_____

_____

_____

TODAY'S SERMON ENCOURAGED ME TO:

_____

_____

_____

TOPIC/TITLE: _____

DATE: _____ SPEAKER: _____

SCRIPTURE: _____

Keyword:	Prayer Requests:
_____	_____
	_____
	_____
	_____

MAIN POINTS OR "WOW!" STATEMENTS:

1
_____
_____
_____
_____
_____

2
_____
_____
_____
_____
_____

3
_____
_____
_____
_____
_____

NOTES:

_____

_____

_____

_____

_____

_____

_____

_____

_____

_____

_____

_____

_____

_____

_____

_____

_____

_____

_____

_____

_____

_____

_____

_____

TODAY'S SERMON ENCOURAGED ME TO:

_____

_____

_____

TOPIC/TITLE: _____

DATE: _____ **SPEAKER:** _____

SCRIPTURE: _____

Keyword:	Prayer Requests:
_____	_____
	_____
	_____
	_____

MAIN POINTS OR "WOW!" STATEMENTS:

1 _____
_____
_____
_____
_____

2 _____
_____
_____
_____
_____

3 _____
_____
_____
_____
_____

NOTES:

_____
_____
_____
_____
_____
_____
_____
_____
_____
_____
_____
_____
_____
_____
_____
_____
_____
_____
_____
_____
_____
_____
_____
_____
_____

TODAY'S SERMON ENCOURAGED ME TO:

_____
_____
_____

TOPIC/TITLE: _____

DATE: _____ **SPEAKER:** _____

SCRIPTURE: _____

Keyword:
_____

Prayer Requests:
_____
_____
_____
_____

MAIN POINTS OR "WOW!" STATEMENTS:

1
_____
_____
_____
_____
_____
_____

2
_____
_____
_____
_____
_____
_____

3
_____
_____
_____
_____
_____
_____

NOTES:

_____

_____

_____

_____

_____

_____

_____

_____

_____

_____

_____

_____

_____

_____

_____

_____

_____

_____

_____

_____

_____

_____

_____

TODAY'S SERMON ENCOURAGED ME TO:

_____

_____

_____

TOPIC/TITLE: _____

DATE: _____ **SPEAKER:** _____

SCRIPTURE: _____

Keyword:	Prayer Requests:
_____	_____ _____ _____ _____

MAIN POINTS OR "WOW!" STATEMENTS:

1 _____
_____
_____
_____
_____

2 _____
_____
_____
_____
_____

3 _____
_____
_____
_____
_____

NOTES:

_____

_____

_____

_____

_____

_____

_____

_____

_____

_____

_____

_____

_____

_____

_____

_____

_____

_____

_____

_____

_____

_____

_____

_____

_____

TODAY'S SERMON ENCOURAGED ME TO:

_____

_____

_____

TOPIC/TITLE: _____

DATE: _____ **SPEAKER:** _____

SCRIPTURE: _____

Keyword:
_____

Prayer Requests:
_____
_____
_____
_____

MAIN POINTS OR "WOW!" STATEMENTS:

1 _____
_____
_____
_____
_____

2 _____
_____
_____
_____
_____

3 _____
_____
_____
_____
_____

NOTES:

_____
_____
_____
_____
_____
_____
_____
_____
_____
_____
_____
_____
_____
_____
_____
_____
_____
_____
_____
_____
_____
_____
_____
_____
_____
_____
_____

TODAY'S SERMON ENCOURAGED ME TO:

_____
_____
_____

TOPIC/TITLE: _____

DATE: _____ **SPEAKER:** _____

SCRIPTURE: _____

Keyword:
_____

Prayer Requests:
_____
_____
_____
_____

MAIN POINTS OR "WOW!" STATEMENTS:

1
_____
_____
_____
_____
_____

2
_____
_____
_____
_____
_____

3
_____
_____
_____
_____
_____

NOTES:

_____

_____

_____

_____

_____

_____

_____

_____

_____

_____

_____

_____

_____

_____

_____

_____

_____

_____

_____

_____

_____

_____

_____

TODAY'S SERMON ENCOURAGED ME TO:

_____

_____

_____

TOPIC/TITLE: _____

DATE: _____ **SPEAKER:** _____

SCRIPTURE: _____

Keyword:

_____

Prayer Requests:

_____
_____
_____
_____

MAIN POINTS OR "WOW!" STATEMENTS:

1
_____
_____
_____
_____
_____

2
_____
_____
_____
_____
_____

3
_____
_____
_____
_____

NOTES:

_____

_____

_____

_____

_____

_____

_____

_____

_____

_____

_____

_____

_____

_____

_____

_____

_____

_____

_____

_____

_____

_____

_____

_____

_____

_____

TODAY'S SERMON ENCOURAGED ME TO:

_____

_____

_____

Topic/Title: _____

Date: _____ Speaker: _____

Scripture: _____

Keyword:

_____

Prayer Requests:

_____
_____
_____
_____

Main Points or "WOW!" Statements:

1

_____
_____
_____
_____
_____

2

_____
_____
_____
_____
_____

3

_____
_____
_____
_____
_____

NOTES:

_____

_____

_____

_____

_____

_____

_____

_____

_____

_____

_____

_____

_____

_____

_____

_____

_____

_____

_____

_____

_____

_____

_____

_____

TODAY'S SERMON ENCOURAGED ME TO:

_____

_____

_____

TOPIC/TITLE: _____

DATE: _____ SPEAKER: _____

SCRIPTURE: _____

Keyword:

_____

Prayer Requests:

_____
_____
_____
_____

MAIN POINTS OR "WOW!" STATEMENTS:

1
_____
_____
_____
_____
_____

2
_____
_____
_____
_____
_____

3
_____
_____
_____
_____
_____

NOTES:

_____

_____

_____

_____

_____

_____

_____

_____

_____

_____

_____

_____

_____

_____

_____

_____

_____

_____

_____

_____

_____

_____

_____

TODAY'S SERMON ENCOURAGED ME TO:

_____

_____

_____

TOPIC/TITLE: _____

DATE: _____ **SPEAKER:** _____

SCRIPTURE: _____

Keyword:

_____

Prayer Requests:

_____
_____
_____
_____

MAIN POINTS OR "WOW!" STATEMENTS:

1

2

3

NOTES:

_____
_____
_____
_____
_____
_____
_____
_____
_____
_____
_____
_____
_____
_____
_____
_____
_____
_____
_____
_____
_____
_____
_____
_____

TODAY'S SERMON ENCOURAGED ME TO:

_____
_____
_____

TOPIC/TITLE: _____

DATE: _____ SPEAKER: _____

SCRIPTURE: _____

Keyword:

_____

Prayer Requests:

_____

_____

_____

_____

MAIN POINTS OR "WOW!" STATEMENTS:

1

_____
_____
_____
_____
_____

2

_____
_____
_____
_____
_____

3

_____
_____
_____
_____
_____

NOTES:

_____

_____

_____

_____

_____

_____

_____

_____

_____

_____

_____

_____

_____

_____

_____

_____

_____

_____

_____

_____

_____

_____

_____

_____

_____

_____

TODAY'S SERMON ENCOURAGED ME TO:

_____

_____

_____

TOPIC/TITLE: _____

DATE: _____ **SPEAKER:** _____

SCRIPTURE: _____

Keyword:
_____

Prayer Requests:
_____
_____
_____
_____

MAIN POINTS OR "WOW!" STATEMENTS:

1 _____
_____
_____
_____
_____
_____

2 _____
_____
_____
_____
_____
_____

3 _____
_____
_____
_____
_____

NOTES:

_____
_____
_____
_____
_____
_____
_____
_____
_____
_____
_____
_____
_____
_____
_____
_____
_____
_____
_____
_____
_____
_____
_____

TODAY'S SERMON ENCOURAGED ME TO:

_____
_____
_____

TOPIC/TITLE: _____

DATE: _____ **SPEAKER:** _____

SCRIPTURE: _____

Keyword:

_____

Prayer Requests:

_____

_____

_____

_____

MAIN POINTS OR "WOW!" STATEMENTS:

1

2

3

NOTES:

_____

_____

_____

_____

_____

_____

_____

_____

_____

_____

_____

_____

_____

_____

_____

_____

_____

_____

_____

_____

_____

_____

_____

_____

TODAY'S SERMON ENCOURAGED ME TO:

_____

_____

_____

TOPIC/TITLE: _____

DATE: _____ **SPEAKER:** _____

SCRIPTURE: _____

Keyword:

_____

Prayer Requests:

_____
_____
_____
_____

MAIN POINTS OR "WOW!" STATEMENTS:

1

_____
_____
_____
_____
_____

2

_____
_____
_____
_____
_____

3

_____
_____
_____
_____
_____

NOTES:

_____

_____

_____

_____

_____

_____

_____

_____

_____

_____

_____

_____

_____

_____

_____

_____

_____

_____

_____

_____

_____

_____

_____

_____

TODAY'S SERMON ENCOURAGED ME TO:

_____

_____

_____

TOPIC/TITLE: _____

DATE: _____ **SPEAKER:** _____

SCRIPTURE: _____

Keyword:

_____

Prayer Requests:

_____
_____
_____
_____

MAIN POINTS OR "WOW!" STATEMENTS:

1

_____
_____
_____
_____
_____
_____

2

_____
_____
_____
_____
_____
_____

3

_____
_____
_____
_____
_____
_____

NOTES:

_____

_____

_____

_____

_____

_____

_____

_____

_____

_____

_____

_____

_____

_____

_____

_____

_____

_____

_____

_____

_____

_____

TODAY'S SERMON ENCOURAGED ME TO:

_____

_____

_____

TOPIC/TITLE: _____

DATE: _____ **SPEAKER:** _____

SCRIPTURE: _____

Keyword:
_____

Prayer Requests:
_____
_____
_____
_____

MAIN POINTS OR "WOW!" STATEMENTS:

1
_____
_____
_____
_____

2
_____
_____
_____
_____

3
_____
_____
_____
_____

NOTES:

_____

_____

_____

_____

_____

_____

_____

_____

_____

_____

_____

_____

_____

_____

_____

_____

_____

_____

_____

_____

_____

_____

_____

_____

_____

_____

_____

_____

TODAY'S SERMON ENCOURAGED ME TO:

_____

_____

_____

TOPIC/TITLE: _____

DATE: _____ **SPEAKER:** _____

SCRIPTURE: _____

Keyword:

_____

Prayer Requests:

_____
_____
_____
_____

MAIN POINTS OR "WOW!" STATEMENTS:

1

_____
_____
_____
_____

2

_____
_____
_____
_____

3

_____
_____
_____
_____

NOTES:

_____
_____
_____
_____
_____
_____
_____
_____
_____
_____
_____
_____
_____
_____
_____
_____
_____
_____
_____
_____
_____
_____
_____
_____
_____
_____

TODAY'S SERMON ENCOURAGED ME TO:

_____
_____
_____

TOPIC/TITLE: _____

DATE: _____ **SPEAKER:** _____

SCRIPTURE: _____

Keyword:	Prayer Requests:
_____	_____
	_____
	_____
	_____

MAIN POINTS OR "WOW!" STATEMENTS:

1 _____
_____
_____
_____
_____
_____

2 _____
_____
_____
_____
_____

3 _____
_____
_____
_____
_____

NOTES:

_____

_____

_____

_____

_____

_____

_____

_____

_____

_____

_____

_____

_____

_____

_____

_____

_____

_____

_____

_____

_____

_____

_____

TODAY'S SERMON ENCOURAGED ME TO:

_____

_____

_____

TOPIC/TITLE: _____

DATE: _____   SPEAKER: _____

SCRIPTURE: _____

Keyword:	Prayer Requests:
_____	_____
	_____
	_____
	_____

MAIN POINTS OR "WOW!" STATEMENTS:

1
_____
_____
_____
_____
_____

2
_____
_____
_____
_____
_____

3
_____
_____
_____
_____
_____

NOTES:

_____

_____

_____

_____

_____

_____

_____

_____

_____

_____

_____

_____

_____

_____

_____

_____

_____

_____

_____

_____

_____

_____

_____

_____

_____

_____

TODAY'S SERMON ENCOURAGED ME TO:

_____

_____

_____

TOPIC/TITLE: _____

DATE: _____ **SPEAKER:** _____

SCRIPTURE: _____

Keyword: _____
_____

Prayer Requests:
_____
_____
_____
_____

MAIN POINTS OR "WOW!" STATEMENTS:

1
_____
_____
_____
_____
_____

2
_____
_____
_____
_____
_____

3
_____
_____
_____
_____
_____

NOTES:

_____
_____
_____
_____
_____
_____
_____
_____
_____
_____
_____
_____
_____
_____
_____
_____
_____
_____
_____
_____
_____
_____
_____
_____

TODAY'S SERMON ENCOURAGED ME TO:

_____
_____
_____

TOPIC/TITLE: _____

DATE: _____ **SPEAKER:** _____

SCRIPTURE: _____

Keyword:
_____

Prayer Requests:
_____
_____
_____
_____

MAIN POINTS OR "WOW!" STATEMENTS:

1
_____
_____
_____
_____
_____
_____

2
_____
_____
_____
_____
_____
_____

3
_____
_____
_____
_____
_____
_____

NOTES:

_____

_____

_____

_____

_____

_____

_____

_____

_____

_____

_____

_____

_____

_____

_____

_____

_____

_____

_____

_____

_____

_____

_____

TODAY'S SERMON ENCOURAGED ME TO:

_____

_____

_____

TOPIC/TITLE: _____

DATE: _____ **SPEAKER:** _____

SCRIPTURE: _____

Keyword:	Prayer Requests:
_____	_____
	_____
	_____
	_____

MAIN POINTS OR "WOW!" STATEMENTS:

1 _____
_____
_____
_____
_____

2 _____
_____
_____
_____
_____

3 _____
_____
_____
_____
_____

NOTES:

_____
_____
_____
_____
_____
_____
_____
_____
_____
_____
_____
_____
_____
_____
_____
_____
_____
_____
_____
_____
_____
_____
_____
_____
_____
_____

TODAY'S SERMON ENCOURAGED ME TO:

_____
_____
_____

TOPIC/TITLE: _____

DATE: _____ **SPEAKER:** _____

SCRIPTURE: _____

Keyword:

_____

Prayer Requests:

_____
_____
_____
_____

MAIN POINTS OR "WOW!" STATEMENTS:

1
_____
_____
_____
_____
_____

2
_____
_____
_____
_____
_____

3
_____
_____
_____
_____
_____

NOTES:

_____
_____
_____
_____
_____
_____
_____
_____
_____
_____
_____
_____
_____
_____
_____
_____
_____
_____
_____
_____
_____
_____
_____
_____
_____
_____

TODAY'S SERMON ENCOURAGED ME TO:

_____
_____
_____

TOPIC/TITLE: _____

DATE: _____ **SPEAKER:** _____

SCRIPTURE: _____

Keyword:	Prayer Requests:
_____	_____
	_____
	_____
	_____

MAIN POINTS OR "WOW!" STATEMENTS:

1
_____
_____
_____
_____
_____

2
_____
_____
_____
_____
_____

3
_____
_____
_____
_____
_____

NOTES:

_____
_____
_____
_____
_____
_____
_____
_____
_____
_____
_____
_____
_____
_____
_____
_____
_____
_____
_____
_____
_____
_____
_____
_____
_____
_____
_____

TODAY'S SERMON ENCOURAGED ME TO:

_____
_____
_____

TOPIC/TITLE: _____

DATE: _____ SPEAKER: _____

SCRIPTURE: _____

Keyword:	Prayer Requests:
_____	_____
	_____
	_____
	_____

MAIN POINTS OR "WOW!" STATEMENTS:

1
_____
_____
_____
_____
_____

2
_____
_____
_____
_____
_____

3
_____
_____
_____
_____
_____

NOTES:

_____

_____

_____

_____

_____

_____

_____

_____

_____

_____

_____

_____

_____

_____

_____

_____

_____

_____

_____

_____

_____

_____

_____

_____

_____

_____

TODAY'S SERMON ENCOURAGED ME TO:

_____

_____

_____

TOPIC/TITLE: _____

DATE: _____ **SPEAKER:** _____

SCRIPTURE: _____

Keyword:
_____

Prayer Requests:
_____
_____
_____
_____

MAIN POINTS OR "WOW!" STATEMENTS:

1
_____
_____
_____
_____
_____

2
_____
_____
_____
_____
_____

3
_____
_____
_____
_____
_____

NOTES:

_____

_____

_____

_____

_____

_____

_____

_____

_____

_____

_____

_____

_____

_____

_____

_____

_____

_____

_____

_____

_____

_____

_____

_____

_____

TODAY'S SERMON ENCOURAGED ME TO:

_____

_____

_____

TOPIC/TITLE: _____

DATE: _____ **SPEAKER:** _____

SCRIPTURE: _____

Keyword:	Prayer Requests:
_____	_____
	_____
	_____
	_____

MAIN POINTS OR "WOW!" STATEMENTS:

1
_____
_____
_____
_____
_____
_____

2
_____
_____
_____
_____
_____
_____

3
_____
_____
_____
_____
_____

NOTES:

_____
_____
_____
_____
_____
_____
_____
_____
_____
_____
_____
_____
_____
_____
_____
_____
_____
_____
_____
_____
_____
_____
_____
_____
_____
_____

TODAY'S SERMON ENCOURAGED ME TO:

_____
_____
_____

TOPIC/TITLE: _____

DATE: _____ **SPEAKER:** _____

SCRIPTURE: _____

Keyword:

_____

Prayer Requests:

_____
_____
_____
_____

MAIN POINTS OR "WOW!" STATEMENTS:

1

2

3

NOTES:

_____

_____

_____

_____

_____

_____

_____

_____

_____

_____

_____

_____

_____

_____

_____

_____

_____

_____

_____

_____

_____

_____

_____

TODAY'S SERMON ENCOURAGED ME TO:

_____

_____

_____

TOPIC/TITLE: _____

DATE: _____ **SPEAKER:** _____

SCRIPTURE: _____

Keyword:	Prayer Requests:
_____	_____
	_____
	_____
	_____

MAIN POINTS OR "WOW!" STATEMENTS:

1 _____
_____
_____
_____
_____

2 _____
_____
_____
_____
_____

3 _____
_____
_____
_____
_____

NOTES:

_____

_____

_____

_____

_____

_____

_____

_____

_____

_____

_____

_____

_____

_____

_____

_____

_____

_____

_____

_____

_____

_____

_____

_____

TODAY'S SERMON ENCOURAGED ME TO:

_____

_____

_____

TOPIC/TITLE: _____

DATE: _____ **SPEAKER:** _____

SCRIPTURE: _____

Keyword:
_____

Prayer Requests:
_____
_____
_____
_____

MAIN POINTS OR "WOW!" STATEMENTS:

1
_____
_____
_____
_____
_____
_____

2
_____
_____
_____
_____
_____
_____

3
_____
_____
_____
_____
_____
_____

NOTES:

_____
_____
_____
_____
_____
_____
_____
_____
_____
_____
_____
_____
_____
_____
_____
_____
_____
_____
_____
_____
_____
_____
_____
_____
_____

TODAY'S SERMON ENCOURAGED ME TO:

_____
_____
_____

TOPIC/TITLE: _____

DATE: _____ SPEAKER: _____

SCRIPTURE: _____

Keyword:

_____

Prayer Requests:
_____
_____
_____
_____

MAIN POINTS OR "WOW!" STATEMENTS:

1
_____
_____
_____
_____
_____

2
_____
_____
_____
_____
_____

3
_____
_____
_____
_____
_____

NOTES:

_____

_____

_____

_____

_____

_____

_____

_____

_____

_____

_____

_____

_____

_____

_____

_____

_____

_____

_____

_____

_____

_____

_____

_____

TODAY'S SERMON ENCOURAGED ME TO:

_____

_____

_____

TOPIC/TITLE: _____

DATE: _____ **SPEAKER:** _____

SCRIPTURE: _____

Keyword: _____

Prayer Requests:
_____
_____
_____
_____

MAIN POINTS OR "WOW!" STATEMENTS:

1
_____
_____
_____
_____
_____

2
_____
_____
_____
_____
_____

3
_____
_____
_____
_____
_____

NOTES:

_____

_____

_____

_____

_____

_____

_____

_____

_____

_____

_____

_____

_____

_____

_____

_____

_____

_____

_____

_____

_____

_____

_____

_____

_____

_____

TODAY'S SERMON ENCOURAGED ME TO:

_____

_____

_____

TOPIC/TITLE: _____

DATE: _____ **SPEAKER:** _____

SCRIPTURE: _____

Keyword:	Prayer Requests:
_____	_____
	_____
	_____
	_____

MAIN POINTS OR "WOW!" STATEMENTS:

1
_____
_____
_____
_____
_____
_____

2
_____
_____
_____
_____
_____
_____

3
_____
_____
_____
_____
_____
_____

NOTES:

_____
_____
_____
_____
_____
_____
_____
_____
_____
_____
_____
_____
_____
_____
_____
_____
_____
_____
_____
_____
_____
_____
_____

TODAY'S SERMON ENCOURAGED ME TO:

_____
_____
_____

TOPIC/TITLE: _____

DATE: _____ **SPEAKER:** _____

SCRIPTURE: _____

Keyword:

_____

Prayer Requests:

_____

_____

_____

_____

MAIN POINTS OR "WOW!" STATEMENTS:

1

_____

_____

_____

_____

_____

2

_____

_____

_____

_____

_____

3

_____

_____

_____

_____

_____

NOTES:

_____

_____

_____

_____

_____

_____

_____

_____

_____

_____

_____

_____

_____

_____

_____

_____

_____

_____

_____

_____

_____

_____

TODAY'S SERMON ENCOURAGED ME TO:

_____

_____

_____

TOPIC/TITLE: _____

DATE: _____ **SPEAKER:** _____

SCRIPTURE: _____

Keyword:

_____

Prayer Requests:

_____
_____
_____
_____

MAIN POINTS OR "WOW!" STATEMENTS:

1
_____
_____
_____
_____
_____

2
_____
_____
_____
_____
_____

3
_____
_____
_____
_____
_____

NOTES:

_____

_____

_____

_____

_____

_____

_____

_____

_____

_____

_____

_____

_____

_____

_____

_____

_____

_____

_____

_____

_____

_____

_____

_____

_____

_____

_____

TODAY'S SERMON ENCOURAGED ME TO:

_____

_____

_____

TOPIC/TITLE: _____

DATE: _____ **SPEAKER:** _____

SCRIPTURE: _____

Keyword:	Prayer Requests:
_____	_____ _____ _____ _____

MAIN POINTS OR "WOW!" STATEMENTS:

1 _____
_____
_____
_____
_____

2 _____
_____
_____
_____
_____

3 _____
_____
_____
_____

NOTES:

_____
_____
_____
_____
_____
_____
_____
_____
_____
_____
_____
_____
_____
_____
_____
_____
_____
_____
_____
_____
_____
_____
_____
_____
_____

TODAY'S SERMON ENCOURAGED ME TO:

_____
_____
_____

TOPIC/TITLE: _____

DATE: _____ **SPEAKER:** _____

SCRIPTURE: _____

Keyword:

_____

Prayer Requests:

_____
_____
_____
_____

MAIN POINTS OR "WOW!" STATEMENTS:

1
_____
_____
_____
_____
_____

2
_____
_____
_____
_____
_____

3
_____
_____
_____
_____
_____

NOTES:

_____

_____

_____

_____

_____

_____

_____

_____

_____

_____

_____

_____

_____

_____

_____

_____

_____

_____

_____

_____

_____

_____

_____

_____

_____

_____

TODAY'S SERMON ENCOURAGED ME TO:

_____

_____

_____

TOPIC/TITLE: _____

DATE: _____ **SPEAKER:** _____

SCRIPTURE: _____

Keyword:	Prayer Requests:
_____	_____
	_____
	_____
	_____

MAIN POINTS OR "WOW!" STATEMENTS:

1
_____
_____
_____
_____
_____

2
_____
_____
_____
_____
_____

3
_____
_____
_____
_____
_____

NOTES:

_____
_____
_____
_____
_____
_____
_____
_____
_____
_____
_____
_____
_____
_____
_____
_____
_____
_____
_____
_____
_____
_____
_____
_____
_____

TODAY'S SERMON ENCOURAGED ME TO:

_____
_____
_____

TOPIC/TITLE: _____

DATE: _____ **SPEAKER:** _____

SCRIPTURE: _____

Keyword: _____

Prayer Requests:
_____
_____
_____
_____

MAIN POINTS OR "WOW!" STATEMENTS:

1
_____
_____
_____
_____
_____
_____

2
_____
_____
_____
_____
_____
_____

3
_____
_____
_____
_____
_____
_____

NOTES:

_____

_____

_____

_____

_____

_____

_____

_____

_____

_____

_____

_____

_____

_____

_____

_____

_____

_____

_____

_____

_____

_____

_____

TODAY'S SERMON ENCOURAGED ME TO:

_____

_____

_____

TOPIC/TITLE: _____

DATE: _____ SPEAKER: _____

SCRIPTURE: _____

Keyword:	Prayer Requests:
_____	_____ _____ _____ _____

MAIN POINTS OR "WOW!" STATEMENTS:

1
_____
_____
_____
_____
_____

2
_____
_____
_____
_____
_____

3
_____
_____
_____
_____
_____

NOTES:

_____
_____
_____
_____
_____
_____
_____
_____
_____
_____
_____
_____
_____
_____
_____
_____
_____
_____
_____
_____
_____
_____
_____

TODAY'S SERMON ENCOURAGED ME TO:

_____
_____
_____

TOPIC/TITLE: _____

DATE: _____ SPEAKER: _____

SCRIPTURE: _____

Keyword:	Prayer Requests:
_____	_____
	_____
	_____
	_____

MAIN POINTS OR "WOW!" STATEMENTS:

1
_____
_____
_____
_____
_____

2
_____
_____
_____
_____
_____

3
_____
_____
_____
_____
_____

NOTES:

_____
_____
_____
_____
_____
_____
_____
_____
_____
_____
_____
_____
_____
_____
_____
_____
_____
_____
_____
_____
_____
_____
_____
_____
_____
_____

TODAY'S SERMON ENCOURAGED ME TO:

_____
_____
_____

TOPIC/TITLE: _____

DATE: _____ **SPEAKER:** _____

SCRIPTURE: _____

Keyword:

_____

Prayer Requests:

_____
_____
_____
_____

MAIN POINTS OR "WOW!" STATEMENTS:

1
_____
_____
_____
_____
_____

2
_____
_____
_____
_____
_____

3
_____
_____
_____
_____
_____

NOTES:

_____

_____

_____

_____

_____

_____

_____

_____

_____

_____

_____

_____

_____

_____

_____

_____

_____

_____

_____

_____

_____

_____

_____

TODAY'S SERMON ENCOURAGED ME TO:

_____

_____

_____

TOPIC/TITLE: _____

DATE: _____ SPEAKER: _____

SCRIPTURE: _____

Keyword:	Prayer Requests:
_____	_____
	_____
	_____
	_____

MAIN POINTS OR "WOW!" STATEMENTS:

1 _____
_____
_____
_____
_____

2 _____
_____
_____
_____
_____

3 _____
_____
_____
_____
_____

NOTES:

_____

_____

_____

_____

_____

_____

_____

_____

_____

_____

_____

_____

_____

_____

_____

_____

_____

_____

_____

_____

_____

_____

_____

_____

TODAY'S SERMON ENCOURAGED ME TO:

_____

_____

_____

TOPIC/TITLE: _____

DATE: _____ SPEAKER: _____

SCRIPTURE: _____

Keyword:

_____

Prayer Requests:

_____
_____
_____
_____

MAIN POINTS OR "WOW!" STATEMENTS:

1

_____
_____
_____
_____
_____

2

_____
_____
_____
_____
_____

3

_____
_____
_____
_____
_____

NOTES:

_____

_____

_____

_____

_____

_____

_____

_____

_____

_____

_____

_____

_____

_____

_____

_____

_____

_____

_____

_____

_____

_____

_____

_____

_____

_____

TODAY'S SERMON ENCOURAGED ME TO:

_____

_____

_____

TOPIC/TITLE: _____

DATE: _____ **SPEAKER:** _____

SCRIPTURE: _____

Keyword:
_____

Prayer Requests:
_____
_____
_____
_____

MAIN POINTS OR "WOW!" STATEMENTS:

1
_____
_____
_____
_____
_____

2
_____
_____
_____
_____
_____

3
_____
_____
_____
_____
_____

NOTES:

_____

_____

_____

_____

_____

_____

_____

_____

_____

_____

_____

_____

_____

_____

_____

_____

_____

_____

_____

_____

_____

_____

_____

_____

_____

TODAY'S SERMON ENCOURAGED ME TO:

_____

_____